Mambas

Richardson, Adel(

Points: 0.5

W9-CYW-801

SNAKES

Mambas

by Adele D. Richardson

Consultants:

The staff of Black Hills Reptile Gardens

Rapid City, South Dakota

CAPSTONE
HIGH-INTEREST
BOOKS

an imprint of Capstone Press
Mankato, Minnesota

Capstone High-Interest Books are published by Capstone Press
151 Good Counsel Drive, P.O. Box 669, Mankato, Minnesota 56002
http://www.capstone-press.com

Library of Congress Cataloging-in-Publication Data
Richardson, Adele, 1966–
  Mambas / by Adele D. Richardson.
   p. cm.—(Snakes)
  Summary: Describes the physical features, habitat, and hunting and mating
methods of mamba snakes.
  Includes bibliographical references (p. 45) and index.
  ISBN 0-7368-2137-6 (hardcover)
  1. Mambas—Juvenile literature. [1. Mambas. 2. Poisonous snakes. 3. Snakes.]
I. Title. II. Snakes (Mankato, Minn.)
QL666.O64R53 2004
597.96'4—dc21   2002155698

Editorial Credits
Tom Adamson, editor; Patrick Dentinger, book designer; Jo Miller, photo researcher

Photo Credits
Cover: East African green mamba, Joe McDonald

Adrian Warren/Last Refuge, Ltd., 30
AnimalsAnimals/Paul Freed, 34
Ann & Rob Simpson, 6
Bruce Coleman Inc./Rod Williams, 12; Norman Owen Tomalin, 15; Tom Brakefield, 40
Corbis/Rob C. Nunnington/Gallo Images, 27; Rod Patterson/Gallo Images, 28; Anthony
    Bannister/Gallo Images, 32; Eric and David Hosking, 39
David Liebman, 36
Index Stock Imagery/Elizabeth DeLansey, 23
Joe McDonald, 10, 16–17, 24, 44
Michael Cardwell/Extreme Wildlife Photography, 8, 18, 21

1 2 3 4 5 6 08 07 06 05 04 03

Table of Contents

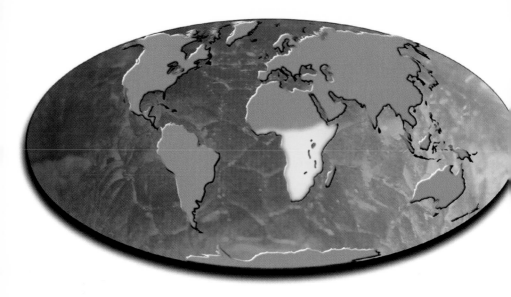

Yellow represents the areas where mambas live.

Fast Facts about Mambas

Scientific Names: Mambas are members of the Elapidae family. They belong to the genus *Dendroaspis*.

Size: Green mambas average about 6 feet (1.8 meters) in length. Black mambas can grow up to 14 feet (4.3 meters) long.

Range: Mambas live in southern and central Africa.

Description:	Mambas have narrow heads and large eyes. Three species of mamba are green. The other species is the black mamba, but its color is not really black. Its scales can be brown, gray, or olive.
Habitat:	Mambas live in forests and savannas. Green mambas spend much of their lives in trees. Black mambas live mostly on the ground. They sometimes climb trees to hunt or to find shelter.
Food:	Mambas eat rodents, birds, and lizards.
Habits:	Mambas kill their prey with venom injected from fangs. Their venom kills prey quickly. Mambas swallow the dead animal whole.
Reproduction:	Females lay up to 15 eggs after mating. In about three months, young mambas hatch from the eggs. They usually are 1 to 2 feet (30 to 61 centimeters) long.

CHAPTER 1

Mambas

Mambas are well known for being dangerous snakes. When threatened, they try to flee. If the snakes cannot escape, they bite to defend themselves. The deadly mamba venom can kill a person within a few hours.

Elapidae Family
Snakes are reptiles, just like turtles, lizards, and alligators. These animals are cold-blooded. Their body temperature changes with their surroundings.

Scientists divide snakes into families. All snakes in a family have similar features. Mambas are part of the Elapidae family.

Mambas are long, slender snakes with large head scales.

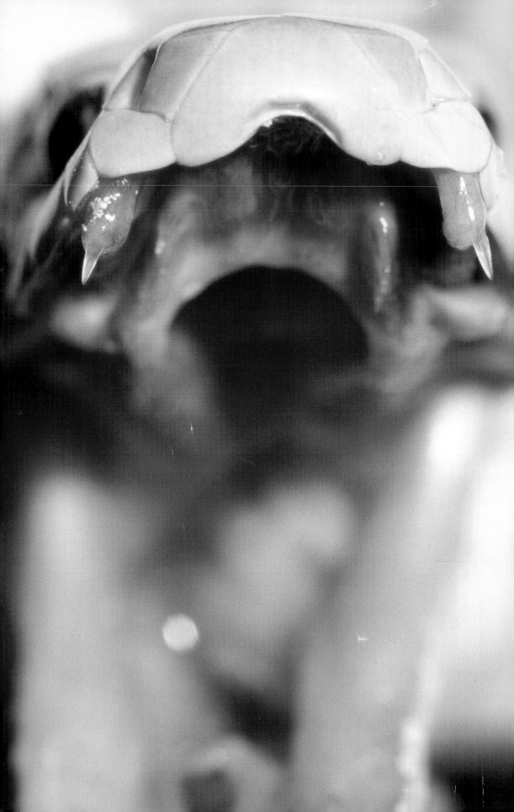

More than 290 species are in this family. Cobras, coral snakes, and sea snakes also belong to this family.

All Elapidae snakes are venomous. They have short fangs at the front of their upper jaws. These teeth are always in the same position. They are called fixed fangs. Venom flows through the fangs and into prey when the snakes bite.

The snake families are divided further into genera. The Elapidae family has about 60 of these smaller groups. Mambas belong to the genus *Dendroaspis*. Within this genus are four species of snakes. They all live in central and southern Africa and are known for producing very powerful venom.

Mamba fangs are small, but they are sharp and deadly.

CHAPTER 2

Mamba Species

All mambas have long, slender bodies covered with smooth scales. They have large eyes and narrow heads. Mambas move easily from branch to branch in trees and shrubs.

There are four species of mambas in the *Dendroaspis* genus. One species is the black mamba. The other three are called green mambas. The green mambas look similar. They have a few small differences in coloring and range.

Black Mamba
The black mamba is one of the largest snakes in Africa. Most adult black mambas are 8 to 9

The black mamba is one of the most feared snakes in Africa.

The West African green mamba has a black outline around each of its scales.

feet (2.4 to 2.7 meters) long. Some of these snakes have grown to 14 feet (4.3 meters) long.

Even though this snake is named black mamba, it is not black. Its scales are brown, gray, or olive. Its underbelly is light gray. This snake earned its name from the deep purple-black color inside its mouth.

The black mamba is the fastest snake in Africa. It can travel along the ground at 7 to 12

MAMBA SPECIES

common name	scientific name
black mamba - *Dendroaspis polylepis*	
eastern green mamba - *Dendroaspis angusticeps*	
Jameson's mamba - *Dendroaspis jamesoni*	
West African green mamba - *Dendroaspis viridis*	

miles (11 to 19 kilometers) per hour. For short distances, this snake can reach 14 miles (23 kilometers) per hour.

West African Green Mamba

The West African green mamba is mostly green. The snake's color changes to yellow near its tail. This species is not as large as the black mamba. Adults grow to an average of 6 to 7 feet (1.8 to 2.1 meters) in length.

The West African green mamba has large scales, especially on its head and down the center of its back. These scales are smooth and dull. Each scale is a shade of blue-green or yellow with a black outline. The outline makes the snake's yellow tail look like a piece of rope.

Jameson's Mamba

The Jameson's mamba is similar to the West African green mamba. This snake can grow to about 6 feet (1.8 meters) long. The Jameson's mamba is mostly green. Each of its scales has a dark outline. The tail of this snake is very dark, almost black. The underbelly of the Jameson's mamba is a lighter shade of green than its back.

Eastern Green Mamba

The eastern green mamba is yellow-green. Its color blends well with tree and shrub leaves. Its underbelly is yellow-white. Like the other mambas, this snake has large head scales. The inside of its mouth is black. Most eastern green mambas are 4 to 7 feet (1.2 to 2.1 meters) long.

The Jameson's mamba looks like the other green mambas, but its tail is very dark.

Large
Head Scales

Outlined
Scales

Eastern Green Mamba

Tail

CHAPTER 3

Habitat

All four species of mambas live in Africa. West African green mambas live in the western part of Africa. These snakes can also be found off the West African coast on São Tomé Island. Eastern green mambas live in most of East Africa. Jameson's mambas are common in western and central Africa, especially near the equator. Black mambas are found mostly in the southern and eastern parts of the continent.

Living in Trees

The three species of green mambas spend much of their lives in trees. Green mambas

Green mambas spend much of their time in trees.

also may spend time in low shrubs. Black mambas spend most of their time on the ground, but they sometimes climb trees.

All mambas can move quickly through trees and shrubs. They have strong muscles that allow them to stretch from branch to branch. Their coloring is good camouflage. Green mambas blend easily with leaves. Black mambas may look the same color as branches.

Mambas' coloring helps them sneak up on animals in trees. They hunt birds or small mammals in trees.

The trees also help warm mambas' bodies. When mambas become cold, they move to a branch in the sun. They stay in the sunlight until their bodies are warm again.

On the Ground

Black mambas spend most of their lives on the ground. They live in savannas and wooded areas. Black mambas sometimes warm their bodies by lying on rocks during the day. They

Black mambas are usually found on the ground.

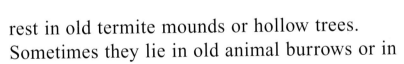

rest in old termite mounds or hollow trees.
Sometimes they lie in old animal burrows or in
piles of rocks.

Green mambas sometimes travel on the
ground. They have to move over land to get to
other trees in open savannas. They also slide

to the ground to eat prey that fell out of a tree. Females sometimes lay eggs in a shelter on the ground.

Predators

Even though mambas are venomous, they do have some predators. Eagles and other birds of prey catch and eat these snakes. The birds swoop down and grab mambas while they lie on tree branches. Sometimes they pick up the snakes lying on rocks or in open savannas. Monitor lizards also eat mambas. These predators are especially dangerous to young mambas.

A ground hornbill will eat young mambas.

CHAPTER 4

Hunting

Like other snakes, mambas are carnivores. They hunt and eat other animals. These snakes usually eat rats, mice, bats, and birds. Mambas will also eat lizards and other snakes.

Hunting Habits

Mambas are diurnal. They are active and hunt during the day, usually in the early morning. When they are not hunting, mambas lie in the sun or rest in a hidden spot.

Mambas often ambush their prey. They stay still for long periods of time and wait for prey to come near. As soon as an animal is close,

When hunting, the black mamba often travels with its head raised up to 18 inches (48 centimeters) off the ground.

mambas strike. If the prey tries to escape, the
snakes quickly follow it.

Senses for Hunting

Mambas' eyes are large and round. Scientists
believe that mambas can see better than most
snakes. They notice the slightest movements
around them.

Mambas do not hear the same way people
do. They use their body to feel sounds. As prey
nears, mambas feel the movement in the
ground or in the trees.

Mambas have an organ on the roof of their
mouth called the Jacobson's organ. Mambas
flick out their tongues often. The tongue
collects scents in the air. The tongue then
carries the scents to the Jacobson's organ.
It helps the snakes find prey.

Killing and Eating Prey

The mamba's powerful venom flows through
short, hollow fangs at the front of its upper
jaw. Mambas bite prey to inject venom into
its body. The venom causes an animal's
muscles to stop working. It quickly affects

Mambas smell for prey with their tongues.

the heart and lungs. Prey dies within minutes
of being bitten.

 Mambas release large animals after biting
them. The prey may try to run, or it may fall
out of a tree. If this happens, the snake follows
the prey's scent to the place where it died.
When striking a smaller animal, a mamba
holds on until the prey's muscles stop

A mamba's powerful venom kills prey. A mamba can swallow prey larger than its head.

working. When the animal stops moving, the snake eats it.

A mamba does not chew its food. Instead, it swallows an animal whole. Prey is usually swallowed headfirst. The prey's legs then fold up neatly inside the mamba's body.

A mamba can swallow prey larger than its head. Its upper and lower jaws are connected with ligaments. This stretchy tissue allows the snake to separate its jaws. Strong muscles then help pull the prey from the snake's throat to its stomach. A mamba's teeth point backward to hold the prey in place while swallowing.

Digesting Food

Besides killing prey, venom helps mambas digest food. Venom is made of powerful digestive juices. These juices break down the prey's body so mambas can use it for energy. The stomach contains more digestive juices. The juices are so strong that they can even break down an animal's bones.

After eating, mambas usually rest. They may rest for a few days or even a few weeks. The length of time depends on the size of the prey. The snakes hunt again soon if the prey was small. Even if the prey was large, mambas do not rest as long as other snakes do. The mambas' active lives make them digest food more quickly.

CHAPTER 5

Mating

Mambas mate during spring or early summer. When females are ready to mate, they give off a scent that male mambas follow. The scent often attracts more than one male. When this happens, the males take part in a combat dance. The winner of the dance will mate with the female.

Combat Dance

The combat dance is a wrestling match between snakes. The dance begins when two males find a female ready to mate. Each male raises its head and the front half of its body. They wrap their bodies around each other.

Male mambas perform a combat dance to determine which one will mate with a female.

Each snake tries to push the other snake to the ground. The winner is usually the bigger, stronger snake. After the weaker snake is held down, the winner lets the weaker snake leave.

The winning snake soon begins courting the female. During courtship, the male flicks his tongue along the female's body. Then the two snakes twist together for mating. They can stay joined for several hours. Mating can last for several days.

Eggs

Mambas are oviparous. The females lay eggs that develop and hatch outside their bodies. The females lay eggs about 40 to 50 days after mating. They usually place the eggs in a pile of rotting plants. Sometimes the eggs are laid in hollow tree stumps. The rotting plants or tree stumps keep the eggs warm.

Females lay between two and 15 eggs at one time. The leathery mamba eggs are long and thin. They average about 2 inches

Mambas hatch from soft, leathery eggs.

(5 centimeters) in length. The young hatch from the eggs about three months later.

The young use an egg tooth to cut an opening in the egg. An egg tooth is a tiny thorn-like spur on a young snake's upper jaw. It falls off soon after hatching.

Young

Newly hatched mambas can be 1 to 2 feet (30 to 61 centimeters) long, depending on the species. They must care for themselves as soon as they hatch. Their mothers do not protect them or bring food. The young find mice or small birds to eat.

Young green mambas look just like the adults. Young black mambas are green-gray. Their skin darkens as they get older. Young black mambas grow quickly. They can grow up to 6 feet (1.8 meters) long within one year.

Young mambas can kill prey just as quickly as the adults. They have fangs and produce deadly venom.

Black mambas are named for the purple-black color inside their mouth.

CHAPTER 6

Mambas and People

Mambas are beautiful but dangerous snakes. Their venom is so strong that less than two drops can kill a person. Even though mambas are dangerous, they are not a great threat to people. They do not prey on people and usually flee if anyone comes near.

Benefits

Mambas provide some benefits to people. They hunt rats and mice. These rodents can spread diseases. The snakes keep rodent populations from growing too large.

Black mambas flatten their necks when they feel threatened.

37

The venom of some mambas is used by scientists to make antivenin. Doctors use it to treat people bitten by mambas. People bitten by mambas will die within a few hours. The antivenin prevents the venom from causing a person's muscles and organs to stop working. Before antivenin was invented, few people ever survived a mamba bite. Zoos that keep mambas have this medicine in case someone is bitten.

Scientists also study black mamba venom for other medical uses. They are trying to make medicines that ease pain and thicken blood. Some people bleed too much when they get even a small cut. These new medicines may help thicken their blood.

Myths

A common myth about snakes is that their skin is slimy. Snakes really have dry, smooth skin.

Some people believe that removing a venomous snake's fangs will make it harmless. This story is not true. In the wild, venomous snakes often lose one or both fangs. When this happens, new fangs soon grow back.

People get venom from mambas for medical uses or to make antivenin.

Another common myth is that mambas chase after people. Mambas are actually shy. When threatened, a mamba first tries to escape. It will strike when a person or predator is too close. But mambas do not hunt people just to bite them.

Eastern green mambas blend well with green leaves.

Defenses

A mamba's best defense is its camouflage. The snake blends in well with its surroundings. A green mamba's color is suited for living in trees. The black mamba blends with tree branches. It also blends with rocks, sticks, and dirt on the ground.

To defend itself, a black mamba raises the front of its body in the air. It can raise its head 3 to 4 feet (.9 to 1.2 meters) high. The snake flattens its head and neck to make a hood similar to a cobra's. It often makes a deep hissing sound. It then shakes its head and opens its mouth wide. If these actions do not scare away an enemy, the snake attacks.

During an attack, a black mamba makes several quick strikes. It can reach an enemy up to 6 feet (1.8 meters) away. As soon as it strikes, the mamba speeds away to its shelter. It stays there until the danger has passed or until it needs to eat again.

Seeing Mambas

Because of these dangers, mambas should never be handled by anyone other than a snake expert. Since mambas are shy, not many people have seen these snakes in the wild.

The best and safest places to see mambas are in zoos. Many zoos throughout the world have mambas. Visitors to zoos can learn about the different species of mambas and how they live.

Words to Know

ambush (AM-bush)—to hide and then attack prey; mambas ambush their prey.

antivenin (ant-ee-VEN-in)—a medicine made from snake venom used to treat snake bites

burrow (BUR-oh)—a hole in the ground often made by an animal

camouflage (KAM-uh-flahzh)—coloring or covering that makes animals, people, or objects look like their surroundings

carnivore (KAR-nuh-vor)—an animal that hunts and eats other animals

digest (dye-JEST)—to break down food so that it can be used by the body

diurnal (dye-UR-nuhl)—active during the day

genus (JEE-nuhss)—a group of plants or animals that are related; genera is the plural of genus.

ligament (LIG-uh-muhnt)—a strong, stretchy band of tissue that connects bones

mammal (MAM-uhl)—a warm-blooded animal with a backbone

oviparous (oh-VIP-uh-rus)—laying eggs that develop and hatch outside the female's body

predator (PRED-uh-tur)—an animal that hunts other animals for food

prey (PRAY)—an animal that is hunted by another animal for food

savanna (suh-VAN-uh)—a flat, grassy area of land with few or no trees

species (SPEE-sheez)—a specific type of plant or animal

venom (VEN-uhm)—a poisonous liquid produced by some snakes, such as mambas

Eastern Green Mamba

To Learn More

Behler, Deborah, and John Behler. *Snakes.* Animalways. New York: Benchmark Books, 2001.

Berger, Melvin, and Gilda Berger. *Can Snakes Crawl Backward?: Questions and Answers about Reptiles.* Scholastic Question and Answer Series. New York: Scholastic Reference, 2001.

Greenaway, Theresa. *Snakes.* The Secret World Of. Austin, Texas: Raintree Steck-Vaughn, 2001.

Mattison, Christopher. *Snake.* New York: DK Publishing, 1999.

Mudd-Ruth, Maria. *Snakes.* Animals, Animals. New York: Marshall Cavendish, 2002.

Useful Addresses

Black Hills Reptile Gardens
P.O. Box 620
Rapid City, SD 57709

Chicago Herpetological Society
2430 North Cannon Drive
Chicago, IL 60614

The Minnesota Herpetological Society
Bell Museum of Natural History
10 Church Street SE
Minneapolis, MN 55455-0104

Toronto Zoo
361A Old Finch Avenue
Scarborough, ON M1B 5K7
Canada

Internet Sites

Do you want to learn more about mambas and other snakes?
Visit the FactHound at *http://www.facthound.com*

FactHound can track down many sites to help you. All the FactHound sites are hand-selected by our editors. FactHound will fetch the best, most accurate information to answer your questions.

IT'S EASY! IT'S FUN!
1) Go to *http://www.facthound.com*
2) Type in: 0736821376
3) Click on "FETCH IT" and FactHound will put you on the trail of several helpful links.

You can also search by subject or book title. So, relax and let our pal FactHound do the research for you!

Index